INNOVATIVE INTEGRITY & VIBRANT VISIONS

EXPLORING GUJARAT'S ETHICAL BUSINESS CULTURE

DR. MINAKSHI BANSAL

DEDICATION

This book is dedicated to the resilient spirit of the people of Gujarat, whose unwavering commitment to ethical values, entrepreneurial drive, and community spirit have shaped the state's vibrant business culture. To the women and men who tirelessly strive for excellence, who honor tradition while embracing innovation, and who understand that true success lies not just in profits, but in making a positive impact on society and the environment. Your dedication to ethical business practices inspires us all and serves as a beacon of hope for a brighter, more sustainable future.

ᐁᐁᐁ

Contents

Contents

Prayer

"Om Bhadram Karnebhih Shrinuyama Devah
Bhadram Pashyemakshabhiryajatrah
Sthirairangais Tushtuvamsastanubhih
Vyashema Devahitam Yadayuh
Svasti Na Indro Vriddhashravah
Svasti Nah Pusha Vishwavedah
Svasti Nastarkshyo Arishtanemih
Svasti No Brihaspatir Dadhatu
Om Shantih Shantih Shantih"

This mantra is a prayer for universal well-being, invoking the blessings of various deities for protection, health, and happiness. It emphasizes the importance of experiencing the auspicious through all senses and living a life aligned with divine purpose. The repetition of "Shantih" at the end signifies a deep desire for peace in the individual, the environment, and the universe at large. This mantra is often recited as a prayer for peace, prosperity, and the physical and spiritual well-being of all beings.

▷▷▷

About The Author

Dr. Minakshi Bansal, born in the bustling metropolis of Delhi, India, has led a life steeped in artistry, scholarly pursuit, and an unwavering commitment to societal betterment. Following her marriage, she relocated to Ahmedabad, Gujarat, where she has since blossomed into a multifaceted beacon of inspiration for many. Dr. Minakshi is not only recognized as a gifted artist in the realm of Fine Arts but also as an esteemed author, a devoted social worker and a dedicated research scholar in Psychology. Her journey, marked by a profound dedication to elevating those around her, especially the downtrodden and underprivileged children of society, is a testament to her deep-seated belief in the transformative power of engagement and empathy.

From her earliest days, Minakshi was distinguished by an insatiable appetite for reading. Her literary universe was inhabited by characters and narratives that spanned ethical tales, motivational and inspirational stories, and the mythic parables imbued with life lessons. This voracious reading habit was not merely for personal edification but was driven by a desire to distill and disseminate the essence of these narratives to foster the development of students and peers alike. She was particularly captivated by the lives and teachings of historical figures and spiritual leaders such as Adi Shankaracharya, Swami Vivekananda, Dr. APJ Abdul Kalam, Mahamana Pandit Madan Mohan Malviya, Mahatma Gandhi, Sardar Vallabhai Patel, and Vinoba Bhave, among others. Their philosophies and life stories fueled her ambition to embody their ideals of resilience, selflessness, and relentless pursuit of knowledge.

Dr. Minakshi's academic and practical engagement with psychology has been equally noteworthy. As a research scholar, her focus has been on exploring the intricate tapestry of the human psyche, aiming to unlock the potential for psychological well-being and societal harmony. Her scholarly work is complemented by her active involvement in social work, where she employs her academic insights to make tangible differences in the lives of the underprivileged. Her endeavours in social work are characterized by an innovative approach that combines traditional wisdom with contemporary psychological practices to address the multifaceted challenges faced by these communities.

Her artistic talents, another facet of her diverse capabilities, are not merely a personal passion but also serve as a medium through which she communicates and connects with others. Her art, rich in symbolism and emotional depth, reflects her philosophical inquiries and social concerns, offering viewers a glimpse into the breadth of her intellect and the depth of her compassion.

In addition to her contributions to the arts and social sciences, Dr. Minakshi has embraced the healing arts of Pranic Healing, mastering the techniques developed by Master Choa Kok Sui. This practice, which focuses on the manipulation of Prana or life energy to heal the body and aura, has been both a personal journey of discovery and a means through which she extends her healing touch to others. Her proficiency in Pranic Healing is complemented by her advocacy and teaching of various forms of meditation aimed at rejuvenation, personal betterment, and the cultivation of harmony within individuals and communities alike.

Dr. Minakshi's life is a narrative of relentless pursuit, not just of personal achievement but of the upliftment and empowerment of society at large. Her diverse interests and talents—spanning the arts, literature, psychology, and the healing practices—converge on a singular path of service. She embodies the spirit of the luminaries who inspired her, channelling their legacy through her actions and teachings. Through her books, art, and social initiatives, she continues to inspire a new generation to embark on their own journeys of self-discovery, resilience, and altruism.

Her commitment to social betterment, particularly her focus on uplifting underprivileged children, reflects a deep understanding of the transformative potential of education and personal development. By integrating her knowledge of psychology, her artistic sensibilities, and her healing practices, Dr. Bansal has developed a holistic approach to social work that addresses both the immediate needs and the long-term well-being of the communities she serves.

As an author, Dr. Minakshi's writings offer a blend of inspirational insights, practical wisdom, and reflective contemplations drawn from her extensive reading and life experiences. Her books serve as a guide for those seeking to navigate the complexities of life with grace, resilience, and purpose. Through her narratives, she extends an invitation to her readers to explore the depths of their own potential and to contribute meaningfully to the collective well-being of society.

In Dr. Minakshi Bansal, we find a remarkable synthesis of the artist, the scholar, the healer, and the social activist. Her life's work stands as a beacon of hope and a source of inspiration for individuals seeking to make a difference in the world. Her story is a compelling reminder of the power of individual action, rooted in compassion and driven by a profound commitment to the betterment of humanity. Dr. Minakshi's legacy is not just in the tangible outcomes of her efforts but in the enduring spirit of inquiry, empathy, and service that she embodies.

ppp

Preface

In a world where business practices are increasingly scrutinized for their ethical dimensions, the pursuit of profits is often viewed through the lens of their impact on society and the environment. This reflection is deeply rooted in a belief that business, beyond generating wealth, has a profound obligation to the communities and worlds it touches. It is within this context that this exploration into Gujarat's business culture becomes not just relevant but necessary.

Gujarat, a vibrant economic powerhouse on India's western frontier, has long been known for its entrepreneurial spirit. The state's history is rich with tales of trade and commerce that date back to ancient times when its ports buzzed with the activities of traders from distant lands. However, what truly makes Gujarat stand out is not just its economic success but the unique blend of traditional values and modern practices that characterize its business ethos.

This exploration began as a journey to understand how businesses in Gujarat have woven ethical practices into their operational tapestry. What does it mean for a business to operate ethically in a competitive global environment? How do traditional values influence modern business practices? These questions were at the heart of countless conversations with business leaders, employees, and stakeholders within Gujarat's diverse economic sectors.

What emerged from these discussions was a fascinating narrative about the integration of age-old cultural practices with contemporary business strategies. In Gujarat, business is not just a commercial activity but a community-oriented endeavor that emphasizes trust, respect, and responsibility. The guiding principles of Jainism and Hinduism, which emphasize non-violence, honesty, and self-regulation, permeate the business environment, influencing decisions and strategies. These principles have not only shaped the ethical frameworks of businesses but have also paved the way for innovative practices that are both sustainable and profitable.

Moreover, the role of women in Gujarat's business culture has been evolving. Traditionally sidelined in the predominantly male-driven business landscape, women are now at the forefront of transforming the state's economic profile. Their stories are not just about success but about overcoming deep-seated challenges and breaking through barriers to forge paths that others can follow.

Sustainability also emerges as a key theme in Gujarat's business practices. In an age where environmental concerns are paramount, the state's businesses have adopted green technologies and practices that point towards a sustainable approach to industrial growth. From renewable energy initiatives to sustainable agricultural practices and water conservation, the businesses here reflect a commitment to the planet that sustains us all.

Another significant aspect of Gujarat's business landscape is its global connectivity. In an increasingly interconnected world, how a business aligns local values with global practices is crucial. Gujarat's businesses demonstrate that it is possible to maintain strong local cultural identities while embracing global market opportunities. This delicate balance is managed through strategic innovations and collaborations that respect cultural heritage while fostering global partnerships.

This book does not merely document these practices; it delves into the ethos that drives them. It seeks to understand the soul of Gujarat's business culture, exploring how ethical considerations are integrated into the fabric of business operations and how these practices impact the broader socio-economic landscape.

The insights gathered here are intended for anyone interested in the confluence of ethics, culture, and business. Whether you are a business professional, an entrepreneur, a student of business ethics, or simply a curious mind, the stories and reflections contained in these pages offer valuable lessons on the sustainable integration of ethical practices in business.

As we move forward in an era where integrity and vision are paramount to sustainable success, Gujarat's example provides a beacon. It shows that at the intersection of tradition and innovation lies a vibrant vision not just for business, but for society as a whole. This book is an invitation to explore this vision, to be inspired by it, and perhaps, to implement its lessons in various contexts around the world, reinforcing the belief that good ethics indeed make for good business.

Dr. Minakshi Bansal
Social Activist
Ahmedabad, Gujarat, Bharat

ONE

The Foundations of Gujarat's Business Ethos

Gujarat's business ethos is deeply rooted in its rich history, vibrant culture, and strong community values, which collectively shape its unique approach to commerce and trade. The entrepreneurial spirit of this region is not a recent development but a continuation of a long-standing tradition that dates back to ancient times when Gujarat was a major center for trade with other parts of Asia, Africa, and the Arab world. This foundational aspect of the state's identity has influenced its modern business practices, emphasizing a blend of innovation, integrity, and a commitment to community welfare.

Historical and Cultural Influences

The business ethos in Gujarat is heavily influenced by the region's history and culture. Historically, Gujaratis have been known for their trade acumen, which is evident from their extensive trading networks that not only spanned the Indian subcontinent but also reached overseas. This trading background has instilled a natural inclination towards business and commerce in the local populace.

Furthermore, the teachings of prominent leaders like Mahatma Gandhi, who led India's independence movement from Gujarat, have left an indelible mark on the business practices in the region. Gandhi's principles of honesty, non-violence, and self-sufficiency resonate strongly in the state's approach to business, encouraging practices that are ethical and socially responsible.

Community and Family Values

Another cornerstone of Gujarat's business ethos is the strong sense of community and family values that permeate its corporate culture. In many Gujarati businesses, especially in the SME sector, enterprises are family-owned and managed, with successive generations contributing to the business. This continuity fosters a culture of loyalty and long-term thinking, rare in more transient corporate environments. The familial approach often extends to how employees are treated, with a greater emphasis on employee welfare and a paternalistic leadership style. These attributes are conducive to creating a stable business environment where long-term relationships with customers and suppliers are valued over short-term gains.

Ethical Practices and Governance

Ethical practices are a hallmark of Gujarati business operations. There is a strong emphasis on fairness, integrity, and transparency in dealings, which

is reinforced by both societal expectations and religious teachings. The majority of Gujarati businesspeople adhere to the principles of Jainism and Hinduism, which advocate for non-violence and ethical behavior in all aspects of life, including business. This religious influence helps to instill a sense of moral responsibility towards the community and the environment, guiding businesses to operate in a manner that is not only profitable but also beneficial to society at large.

Innovation and Adaptation

While rooted in tradition, Gujarati businesses are also known for their adaptability and innovation. This region has been at the forefront of several industrial revolutions in India, from the textile mills of the early 20th century to the diamond polishing factories and the booming tech startups of today. The ability to innovate within the confines of traditional ethical values is a unique characteristic of Gujarat's business culture. This innovative spirit is supported by a robust educational system and a network of institutions that foster entrepreneurship, providing a steady stream of skilled professionals and innovative thinkers.

Sustainability and Social Responsibility

In recent years, there has been a growing emphasis on sustainability and social responsibility among Gujarati businesses. This shift is partly due to global trends but also stems from a deep-seated respect for the environment that is embedded in local culture. Gujarati companies are increasingly adopting green technologies and practices, and are involved in community welfare projects that enhance their corporate social responsibility. Projects such as water conservation, education for underprivileged children, and supporting rural development are common among large and small enterprises alike.

The business ethos of Gujarat is a unique blend of ancient traditions and modern entrepreneurial practices. It is characterized by a strong commitment to ethical values, community welfare, and innovation. This ethos not only defines the business landscape of Gujarat but also sets a model for others to follow, contributing to the overall socio-economic development of the region and positioning Gujarat as a leader in ethical and sustainable business practices on a global stage. As Gujarat continues to evolve, these foundational elements remain steadfast, guiding its journey towards future growth and success.

❦❦❦

"In Gujarat, tradition is not just a relic of the past;
it's the cornerstone of modern business, where
ancient values guide contemporary
entrepreneurship towards a brighter future."

᭬᭬᭬

TWO

HISTORICAL INFLUENCES ON MODERN BUSINESS PRACTICES

Gujarat's modern business practices are deeply rooted in a historical context that is rich with trade, innovation, and cultural exchange. The region's strategic location on the western coast of India made it an active participant in the maritime activities of the past, facilitating trade with regions as diverse as the Middle East, Southeast Asia, and East Africa. This historical backdrop has not only shaped the business landscape of Gujarat but also ingrained a deep-seated mercantile spirit among its people, influencing contemporary business practices.

The Legacy of Maritime Trade

The legacy of Gujarat's maritime trade begins with its ancient ports like Lothal, which was one of the southernmost outposts of the Indus Valley Civilization. Archaeological evidence suggests that Lothal had a sophisticated dockyard, which played a pivotal role in fostering trade relations with the ancient civilizations of Egypt, Mesopotamia, and Persia. This early exposure to international trade laid the foundation for a culture that valued trade and commerce. The skills, practices, and international connections developed through these early trade interactions helped to cultivate a business acumen that is evident in the entrepreneurial spirit of modern Gujarati businesses.

The Silk Route and Spice Trade

During the medieval period, Gujarat emerged as a prominent center on the Silk Route. The region's textile products, particularly its silks and cottons, were in high demand along the trade routes of Asia, making it a bustling hub of economic activity. Additionally, Gujarat played a crucial role in the spice trade, acting as an intermediary that facilitated the movement of spices from the East to the markets of Europe and the Middle East. This historical role as a trade intermediary honed the negotiation skills of Gujarati traders, skills that are apparent today in the dealings of modern Gujarati businesses. They are known for their ability to negotiate favorable terms and navigate complex international trade regulations.

Influence of Colonial and Post-Colonial Economic Policies

The colonial period introduced new dynamics into the business practices in Gujarat. Under British rule, the region became an important administrative and shipbuilding center. The British also established a number of textile mills in Gujarat, which helped to modernize the industry with new technologies and practices. These changes brought about a shift in the local economy from primarily agrarian to industrial. In the post-colonial era, as India pursued policies of economic self-sufficiency and later economic liberalization, Gujarat was quick to adapt to the changing policies. Today, this adaptability is reflected in how quickly Gujarati businesses can pivot their strategies in response to global economic shifts.

Ethical Foundations and Business Practices

The ethical dimensions of business practices in Gujarat are influenced by the teachings of Mahatma Gandhi, who hails from the region. His principles of non-violence, truthfulness, and self-reliance have deeply influenced the business ethics in Gujarat. For instance, the concept of 'trust-based banking' that emerged in the diamond trading community and the cooperative movement in the dairy industry are reflective of these Gandhian values. These movements emphasize ethical practices, fair trade, and community welfare, setting them apart from purely profit-driven models.

Modern Adaptations and Innovations

In contemporary times, Gujarat continues to be a leader in various sectors such as pharmaceuticals, petrochemicals, and information technology, building on its historical legacy of innovation and trade acumen. The state's ability to blend traditional business practices with modern innovations is a key factor in its success. For example, the modern diamond cutting and polishing industry in Gujarat, which dominates the global market, is a direct descendant of the traditional jewelry and craftsmanship skills that have been prevalent in the region for centuries.

As Gujarat moves forward, the interplay of its rich historical influences with modern business strategies continues to shape its economic landscape. These influences not only provide a competitive edge but also ensure that the growth is sustainable and inclusive. By marrying its past with the present, Gujarat sets an exemplary model of how historical influences can be leveraged to enhance modern business practices.

▷▷▷

"Ethical business practices in Gujarat aren't just about profit margins; they're a testament to the enduring commitment to integrity that defines the state's entrepreneurial spirit."

❦❦❦

THREE

Family-Owned Enterprises: Tradition Meets Modernity

Family-owned enterprises form the backbone of Gujarat's economy, embodying a seamless blend of tradition and modernity. These businesses, often passed down through generations, not only represent a significant portion of the state's economic activity but also exemplify the unique integration of age-old familial loyalty with contemporary business practices. This dual nature fosters environments where respect for tradition coexists with a keenness for innovation, driving economic growth and community development.

The Role of Family in Gujarati Business Culture

In Gujarat, family businesses are prevalent across various sectors, from small shops to large industrial firms. The strong familial structure in Gujarati society supports these enterprises, where business skills and knowledge are passed from one generation to the next. This transfer of knowledge is not just about business acumen but also encompasses the family's values, ethics, and commitment to the community. The continuity provided by familial succession often results in a deep understanding of the business and its market, creating stability and resilience that might elude more transient management structures.

Balancing Tradition with Modern Business Demands

The challenge for many family-owned businesses in Gujarat lies in balancing respect for traditional practices with the demands of a rapidly changing global economy. For instance, while older generations might prefer traditional approaches to business management and customer relations, younger family members often bring new ideas, technologies, and practices that can enhance competitiveness and efficiency. Embracing digital technology, modern marketing strategies, and international business standards without losing the essence of their traditional values is a critical balance that many Gujarati family businesses strive to achieve.

Succession Planning and Professional Management

Succession planning represents a critical juncture for family-owned businesses, with the potential to make or break the enterprise. In Gujarat, where family and business ties are often deeply intertwined, the process of handing over control from one generation to the next can be complex. Increasingly, families are recognizing the need for incorporating external professional management into their businesses to complement family members' expertise. This approach helps in professionalizing the business, bringing in fresh perspectives, and ensuring that the company can thrive in competitive markets without losing its familial identity.

Innovation within the Family Business

Innovation is key to the evolution and sustainability of family-owned businesses in Gujarat. Many such enterprises have pioneered sectors like diamond cutting, textiles, and manufacturing by innovating within their traditional business models. For example, diamond businesses in Surat have adopted advanced technologies for cutting and polishing that have set global standards. Similarly, textile businesses in Ahmedabad have innovated with designs and sustainable practices that have redefined the market. These innovations are often driven by the younger members of the family, who bring in new skills and ideas gained through formal education and exposure to global trends.

Community Engagement and Corporate Responsibility

Family-owned businesses in Gujarat are notably involved in community welfare and social initiatives. This commitment is rooted in the Gujarati ethos of giving back to the community that supports the business. Many businesses run charitable trusts, sponsor educational programs, and engage in health and welfare initiatives that benefit their local communities. This social responsibility is often a reflection of the family's values and is an integral part of the business's identity.

As family-owned businesses in Gujarat navigate the complexities of the modern economy, they continue to thrive by leveraging their inherent strengths—deep market knowledge, strong community ties, and flexible management. These businesses are not just surviving but are thriving by effectively bridging the gap between tradition and modernity, ensuring that they remain relevant and resilient in the face of evolving global challenges. This blend of the old and the new underpins the dynamic nature of Gujarat's economy and is a model for family-owned enterprises worldwide, demonstrating how deep-rooted values can harmonize with innovative practices to create enduring and prosperous business legacies.

❦❦❦

"From family-owned enterprises to global corporations, Gujarat's business landscape is a tapestry of tradition and innovation, woven together by a shared dedication to ethical principles."

❦❦❦

FOUR

CORPORATE GOVERNANCE IN GUJARAT'S INDUSTRIES

Corporate governance in Gujarat's industries represents a critical aspect of business operations, reflecting a unique blend of traditional values and modern regulatory frameworks. In Gujarat, as in the rest of India, corporate governance involves a set of practices and procedures that are designed to ensure accountability, fairness, and transparency in a business's relationship with its various stakeholders, including shareholders, customers, and the wider community. This framework not only enhances business integrity and efficiency but also plays a pivotal role in sustaining economic growth and maintaining investor confidence.

The Regulatory Framework and Its Impact

The corporate governance landscape in Gujarat is shaped by both national and state-specific regulations. The Companies Act of India provides a basic framework, which is supplemented by guidelines issued by the Securities and Exchange Board of India (SEBI). These regulations are designed to prevent fraud and mismanagement, ensuring that businesses operate in a transparent and ethical manner. For Gujarat's industries, adherence to these regulations is critical for maintaining business legitimacy and accessing capital markets both domestically and internationally.

Gujarat's businesses often exceed compliance with these regulatory frameworks, driven by a culture that values trust and ethical practices. This is particularly evident in the numerous family-run businesses that dominate the state's industrial landscape, where reputation and personal integrity play a significant role in business operations.

The Role of Independent Directors

One of the key aspects of good corporate governance is the role of independent directors. These individuals are meant to act as a safeguard for shareholders, ensuring that the company's management acts in the best interests of the shareholders and the company as a whole. In Gujarat, the inclusion of independent directors has been a growing trend, especially in publicly listed companies where scrutiny is higher. These directors bring impartiality and expertise, often helping companies navigate complex business challenges and enhancing their strategic decision-making processes.

Transparency and Accountability

Transparency and accountability are cornerstone principles of corporate governance, and in Gujarat, these principles are taken very seriously. Companies are expected to regularly disclose financial reports, management decisions, and other important information in a timely and accurate manner. This transparency is essential for maintaining trust among investors and the public, and it also serves to strengthen the governance structures within companies by discouraging fraudulent or unethical behavior.

Gujarat's industries, particularly those in sectors like pharmaceuticals, chemicals, and energy, have often been at the forefront of adopting international best practices in reporting and transparency. This is not just due to regulatory requirements but also a result of the global nature of these businesses, which necessitates adherence to international standards to attract foreign partnerships and investments.

Ethical Practices and Corporate Culture

In Gujarat, the emphasis on ethical practices extends beyond mere compliance with laws and regulations. There is a strong cultural emphasis on conducting business in a manner that is fair and just, rooted in the region's strong religious and ethical traditions. This cultural ethos influences corporate governance by encouraging businesses to take a long-term view of their operations, focusing on sustainable practices and ethical dealings with all stakeholders.

Corporate culture in Gujarat often reflects these values, with many companies instituting their own codes of conduct and ethics programs to guide employee behavior and decision-making. These programs are not only about adhering to legal standards but also about building a corporate identity that aligns with the values of honesty, integrity, and responsibility.

Challenges and Future Directions

While Gujarat's industries generally exhibit strong adherence to corporate governance norms, there are challenges. Issues such as family control, which can sometimes hinder transparency and accountability, are prevalent. Moreover, as the global business environment becomes more complex, keeping up with international governance standards requires constant vigilance and adaptation.

The future of corporate governance in Gujarat's industries likely involves a greater integration of technology in governance practices, such as the use of blockchain for enhanced security and transparency in transactions. Additionally, there is a growing emphasis on environmental, social, and governance (ESG) criteria, which are becoming crucial in shaping corporate strategies and investor decisions.

As industries in Gujarat continue to expand and integrate into the global economy, robust corporate governance will remain a critical factor in their success, ensuring that they remain competitive and continue to attract investment from around the world. This commitment to governance, rooted in a blend of traditional values and modern practices, positions Gujarat's industries well for future challenges and opportunities.

ᠹᠹᠹ

"Sustainability isn't just a buzzword in Gujarat; it's a way of life, where businesses embrace eco-friendly practices that ensure prosperity for future generations."

❥❥❥

FIVE

SUSTAINABILITY INITIATIVES AND GREEN BUSINESS"

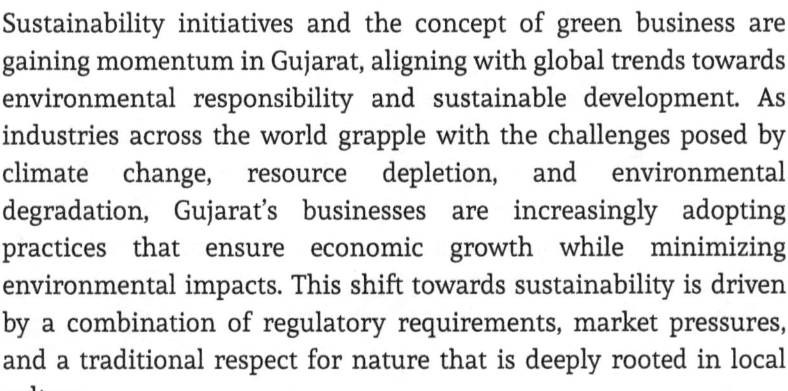

Sustainability initiatives and the concept of green business are gaining momentum in Gujarat, aligning with global trends towards environmental responsibility and sustainable development. As industries across the world grapple with the challenges posed by climate change, resource depletion, and environmental degradation, Gujarat's businesses are increasingly adopting practices that ensure economic growth while minimizing environmental impacts. This shift towards sustainability is driven by a combination of regulatory requirements, market pressures, and a traditional respect for nature that is deeply rooted in local culture.

Driving Forces Behind Sustainability in Gujarat

The push towards green business practices in Gujarat is influenced by several factors. Regulatory frameworks at both the national and state levels have been pivotal in encouraging industries to adopt sustainable practices. Policies promoting renewable energy, waste management, and water conservation have set the stage for businesses to innovate in their processes and products. Moreover, Gujarat's government has been proactive in attracting investments in solar and wind energy, making it a hub for renewable energy projects in India.

Apart from regulatory drivers, consumer awareness and demands for environmentally friendly products have also prompted businesses to adopt green practices. This is particularly evident in sectors such as textiles and manufacturing, where sustainable products often fetch a premium in both domestic and international markets. Additionally, the investment community is increasingly factoring in environmental, social, and governance (ESG) criteria into their investment decisions, which further incentivizes companies to improve their sustainability credentials.

Innovations in Green Technology

Innovation is at the heart of the transition towards green businesses in Gujarat. The state has become a pioneer in various green technologies, especially in the fields of solar energy, wind energy, and water purification technologies. Gujarat was one of the first states in India to develop a solar policy and has since established one of the largest solar parks in the world. This not only helps in reducing the carbon footprint of the state but also serves as a model for other regions.

Similarly, Gujarat's industries are investing in new technologies that reduce water use and improve water management. The textile industry, which is traditionally water-intensive, has seen significant advancements with the introduction of water-saving dyeing processes and wastewater treatment facilities that recycle water for industrial use.

Sustainable Supply Chains

Building sustainable supply chains is another critical aspect where Gujarat's industries are making significant strides. From sourcing raw materials responsibly to optimizing logistics to reduce carbon emissions, companies are rethinking their supply chains to enhance sustainability. This involves close collaboration with suppliers to ensure they also adhere to sustainable practices, thus extending the impact of green initiatives beyond the immediate operations of a single company.

For example, the diamond industry in Surat, which is a major hub for diamond cutting and polishing, is increasingly adopting practices that ensure the ethical sourcing of diamonds and reduce the environmental impact of its operations. This includes investments in technology that improves the efficiency of the cutting and polishing process, thus reducing waste and energy consumption.

Challenges and Adaptations

While there is a strong move towards sustainability, Gujarat's industries face several challenges in fully implementing green business practices. The initial cost of adopting new technologies and processes can be high, and there can be resistance within organizations accustomed to traditional ways of operating. Moreover, balancing economic growth with environmental sustainability continues to be a complex challenge, particularly in sectors that are inherently resource-intensive.

To address these challenges, many companies in Gujarat are engaging in partnerships with global firms that bring in expertise and technology aimed at enhancing sustainability. These collaborations are proving crucial in overcoming technical and financial hurdles associated with green initiatives.

As Gujarat's industries continue to evolve, the integration of sustainability into business strategies is becoming increasingly important. This integration not only ensures compliance with global standards but also enhances the competitiveness of businesses in the global market. By continuing to innovate and adapt, Gujarat sets an example for sustainable industrial growth that other regions in India and around the world can follow. This commitment to green business practices reflects a broader recognition of the need to sustain not just economic growth but also the environmental and social foundations that support it.

ᐁᐁᐁ

"In Gujarat, the diamond industry isn't just about
dazzling gems; it's a shining example of ethical
sourcing and transparent trade practices that set
global standards."

❦❦❦

SIX

CRAFTING CULTURES OF TRANSPARENCY AND TRUST

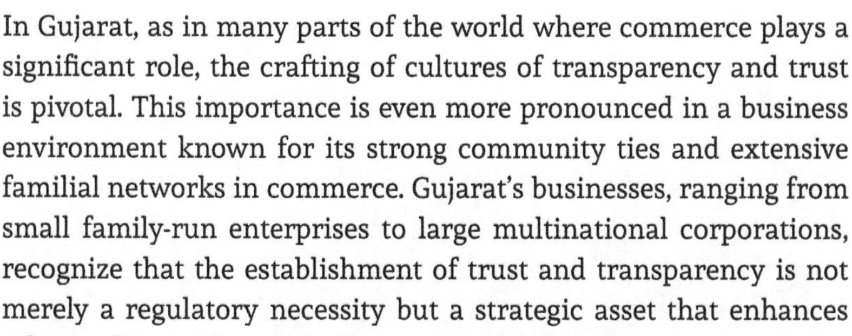

In Gujarat, as in many parts of the world where commerce plays a significant role, the crafting of cultures of transparency and trust is pivotal. This importance is even more pronounced in a business environment known for its strong community ties and extensive familial networks in commerce. Gujarat's businesses, ranging from small family-run enterprises to large multinational corporations, recognize that the establishment of trust and transparency is not merely a regulatory necessity but a strategic asset that enhances relationships with stakeholders and builds lasting success.

The Importance of Trust and Transparency

Trust and transparency in business practices are essential for creating a favorable business environment that attracts investments and fosters sustainable growth. In Gujarat, this is particularly true as the state's economy is heavily reliant on trade and industry. A culture of openness and honesty not only facilitates smoother transactions but also mitigates risks by ensuring that all parties in a business transaction have access to the same information, thereby reducing the likelihood of disputes.

Transparency is crucial in cultivating trust among all stakeholders, including investors, employees, customers, and the community at large. When stakeholders feel that they are receiving honest and complete information, their confidence in the business increases. This confidence, in turn, can lead to more robust business relationships, easier access to capital, and a more resilient reputation.

Historical and Cultural Foundations of Trust

The cultural context of Gujarat, with its emphasis on community and family values, greatly enhances its business practices. Historically, Gujarat has been a major trading center where business was often conducted based on verbal agreements and handshakes. Even today, in many traditional sectors, business deals are sealed with little more than a promise, underscoring the high level of trust that characterizes transactions.

Moreover, the influence of religious and spiritual traditions, such as Jainism and Hinduism, which promote ethical behavior and integrity, has seeped into business practices. The ethical mandates from these religious teachings encourage business leaders to maintain a high standard of honesty and ethical behavior, which in turn fosters a culture of trust.

Building Transparency through Technology

In contemporary times, technology plays a pivotal role in enhancing transparency in Gujarat's businesses. The adoption of modern information and communication technologies allows companies to disseminate information quickly and efficiently, ensuring that all stakeholders are well-informed. Technologies such as blockchain and advanced data analytics are being employed to provide a transparent, immutable record of transactions, enhancing trust particularly in industries like finance and gemstone trading, where the provenance and authenticity of products are critical.

Moreover, technology facilitates regulatory compliance more effectively by automating reporting processes and making them more accurate and timely. This not only helps businesses keep up with the often complex regulatory environment but also assures stakeholders that the business is adhering to all legal and ethical standards.

Institutionalizing Transparency

For many organizations in Gujarat, transparency is institutionalized through robust corporate governance frameworks. These frameworks are designed to ensure that all actions taken by the company are aligned with the best interests of all stakeholders and comply with regulatory requirements. Corporate governance mechanisms such as audits, compliance programs, and board oversight are integral in building a transparent organizational culture.

Furthermore, many Gujarati companies are adopting international best practices and standards, which often require rigorous transparency and accountability measures. By aligning with these global standards, businesses not only improve their operations domestically but also position themselves as trustworthy partners in the international marketplace.

Challenges and Strategies for Enhancing Trust

Despite the high value placed on transparency and trust, businesses in Gujarat face challenges in fully implementing these principles. Issues such as corruption, nepotism, and informal business practices can undermine efforts to build transparency and trust. To combat these challenges, many forward-thinking businesses in Gujarat are investing in ethics training for their employees, establishing clear whistleblowing policies, and engaging in regular audits and assessments to ensure compliance with ethical standards.

The crafting of cultures of transparency and trust in Gujarat's businesses is a dynamic and ongoing process. As the business environment becomes increasingly complex and interconnected, the ability of companies to maintain high standards of openness and integrity will be crucial in navigating future challenges. By continuing to invest in ethical practices, technology, and robust governance frameworks, Gujarat's businesses not only enhance their operational efficiency but also contribute to the overall health and sustainability of the global economic system.

ᐅᐅᐅ

"Tourism in Gujarat isn't just about sightseeing; it's
a journey of responsible exploration, where
travelers connect with communities and preserve
the state's cultural heritage."

❧❧❧

SEVEN

INNOVATION IN TEXTILES: A SUSTAINABLE APPROACH

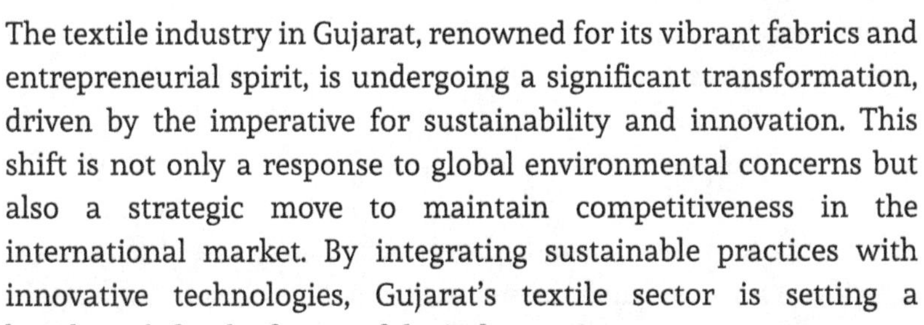

The textile industry in Gujarat, renowned for its vibrant fabrics and entrepreneurial spirit, is undergoing a significant transformation, driven by the imperative for sustainability and innovation. This shift is not only a response to global environmental concerns but also a strategic move to maintain competitiveness in the international market. By integrating sustainable practices with innovative technologies, Gujarat's textile sector is setting a benchmark for the future of the industry.

Historical Significance and Current Innovations

Gujarat has been at the forefront of textile production in India for centuries, known for its diverse fabric types and intricate designs, including the famous Bandhani tie-dye and Patola silk weaves. This rich heritage provides a strong foundation for the industry, which today is bolstered by modern innovations aimed at reducing environmental impact and enhancing production efficiency.

The adoption of sustainable practices in the textile sector is primarily focused on reducing water consumption, minimizing chemical use, and lowering energy requirements. Innovations such as waterless dyeing technologies and the use of organic materials are becoming increasingly prevalent, reflecting a commitment to environmental stewardship that aligns with global sustainability trends.

Water Conservation Techniques

Water is a critical resource in textile manufacturing, used extensively in dyeing and finishing processes. Gujarat's textile businesses are pioneering water conservation measures to address this issue. Techniques like low-liquor ratio dyeing machines and air-dye technology, which significantly reduce the amount of water required for dyeing, are examples of how the industry is innovating to preserve this vital resource. Additionally, many factories are implementing water recycling systems that allow them to reuse wastewater, thus reducing their overall water consumption.

Chemical Management and Reduction

The textile industry is also known for its heavy use of chemicals, which can have detrimental environmental and health impacts. In response, Gujarat's textile manufacturers are exploring the use of natural dyes and mordants, which not only reduce the chemical load but also offer the added benefit of creating unique colors and finishes that are highly valued in the fashion industry. Moreover, the adoption of closed-loop chemical systems ensures that chemicals are recycled within the production processes, minimizing waste and exposure.

Energy Efficiency and Renewable Energy

Energy efficiency is another area where Gujarat's textile industry is focusing its innovative efforts. The adoption of energy-efficient machinery and optimization of energy use in production processes are common strategies. Moreover, many textile units in Gujarat are transitioning to renewable energy sources, such as solar and wind power, to mitigate their carbon footprint. This not only helps in reducing environmental impact but also enhances the industry's sustainability profile, which is increasingly important to global consumers and partners.

Integrating Traditional Techniques with Modern Innovations

One of the unique aspects of Gujarat's approach to sustainable textile production is its integration of traditional handicraft techniques with modern technologies. This integration preserves cultural heritage while enhancing product value and appeal. For example, artisans are using traditional methods like handlooming and block printing in conjunction with eco-friendly dyes and sustainable fabrics to produce high-quality, sustainable products that cater to a niche market.

Collaborative Efforts and Policy Support

The transformation towards sustainable textile manufacturing is supported by collaborative efforts between the government, industry associations, and research institutions. Policies that encourage sustainable practices through subsidies, tax breaks, and technical support are crucial in this transition. Additionally, Gujarat's textile industry benefits from collaborations with international bodies that provide expertise and funding for sustainability projects.

Challenges and Future Prospects

Despite the progress, the journey towards complete sustainability in textile manufacturing is fraught with challenges. The high cost of adopting new technologies, resistance to change in traditional business practices, and market competition from less sustainable but cheaper alternatives pose significant hurdles. However, the long-term benefits of sustainable practices—such as reduced environmental impact, enhanced brand reputation, and compliance with international environmental standards—provide compelling reasons for continued investment and innovation in this area.

As the global textile market continues to evolve, Gujarat's textile industry is well-positioned to lead by example in sustainable manufacturing. By leveraging its historical strengths and embracing innovation, the sector not only ensures its own sustainability but also contributes to the broader goal of environmental conservation. This proactive approach is likely to pave the way for new opportunities and continued growth, establishing Gujarat as a hub for sustainable textile production on the global stage.

ᏤᏤᏤ

"Women entrepreneurs in Gujarat aren't just
breaking glass ceilings; they're shattering
stereotypes and paving the way for a more inclusive
and equitable business landscape."

❥❥❥

EIGHT

WOMEN ENTREPRENEURS IN GUJARAT'S BUSINESS LANDSCAPE

In Gujarat's dynamic business landscape, women entrepreneurs are increasingly prominent, carving out substantial niches in various industries and contributing significantly to the state's economic development. This surge in female entrepreneurship reflects broader social changes and the progressive policies that have been implemented to encourage women in business. Despite facing traditional challenges, these women are redefining the entrepreneurial environment in Gujarat through innovation, resilience, and a strong sense of community and ethical responsibility.

The Rise of Women Entrepreneurs

The increasing visibility of women entrepreneurs in Gujarat is a testament to the state's evolving economic and social fabric. Traditionally, women's involvement in business was often limited to family-run enterprises, without acknowledgment of their roles as decision-makers or innovators. Today, however, more women are founding startups, leading large corporations, and transforming family businesses with modern management practices and new technologies.

This shift is supported by several factors, including improved access to education, progressive government policies, and a growing network of support systems such as women's business associations, self-help groups, and professional networks. These platforms provide women with the resources, mentorship, and networking opportunities needed to launch and sustain successful businesses.

Overcoming Barriers

Despite the supportive ecosystem, women entrepreneurs in Gujarat still face significant barriers. Societal expectations, gender biases, and the challenge of balancing work and family life are substantial obstacles. Access to finance is another critical hurdle, as women often struggle more than their male counterparts to secure funding from banks and investors, who sometimes doubt their credibility and commitment to long-term business ventures.

However, many women entrepreneurs are overcoming these barriers through innovative business models and strategies. For instance, leveraging technology has enabled them to work flexibly and manage businesses remotely. Furthermore, women are increasingly visible in sectors traditionally dominated by men, such as manufacturing, IT, and energy, breaking stereotypes and paving the way for more inclusive industry practices.

Impact on the Economy and Society

The impact of women entrepreneurs on Gujarat's economy is profound. By starting and scaling businesses, women not only contribute to the state's GDP but also create jobs and foster community development. Their businesses often prioritize social responsibility, focusing on solving local problems, improving education, and enhancing healthcare, which contributes to broader societal benefits.

Moreover, women entrepreneurs in Gujarat tend to reinvest a significant portion of their earnings back into their communities and families, further amplifying their impact on economic and social development. This reinvestment helps improve living standards and education levels, contributing to a cycle of prosperity that benefits future generations.

Success Stories and Role Models

The narrative of women's entrepreneurship in Gujarat is rich with success stories that serve as inspiration. From textile giants and diamond magnates to tech startups and biotech firms, women are at the helm of a diverse range of ventures. These success stories not only highlight the economic potential of women-led businesses but also help change societal attitudes towards women in leadership roles.

Role models play a critical part in this transformative journey. Established women entrepreneurs often mentor younger women, helping them navigate the challenges of the business world. These role models are crucial for building confidence among aspiring female entrepreneurs and demonstrating that women can lead successful, growth-oriented businesses.

Future Prospects

Looking forward, the prospects for women entrepreneurs in Gujarat are promising. As societal attitudes continue to evolve and more targeted support initiatives are implemented, it is likely that the number of women-led businesses will continue to rise. This growth will be supported by ongoing advancements in technology, which provide new opportunities for business innovation and market expansion.

In addition, continuous advocacy for gender equality in business funding, leadership opportunities, and legal rights will be essential to ensure that women can compete on an equal footing in Gujarat's business landscape. With sustained effort and support, women entrepreneurs will not only thrive but also lead the way in transforming Gujarat into a more inclusive, innovative, and economically robust society.

As Gujarat continues to foster a supportive ecosystem for women entrepreneurs, it stands as a beacon of progress, demonstrating how empowering women can lead to more robust economic growth and a more equitable society. The journey of women entrepreneurs in Gujarat is not just about business success; it is about shaping a future where economic opportunities are accessible to all, regardless of gender.

ppp

"Innovation in Gujarat isn't just about cutting-edge technology; it's about finding creative solutions to age-old challenges and driving sustainable growth."

❦❦❦

NINE

Ethical Challenges in the Digital Age

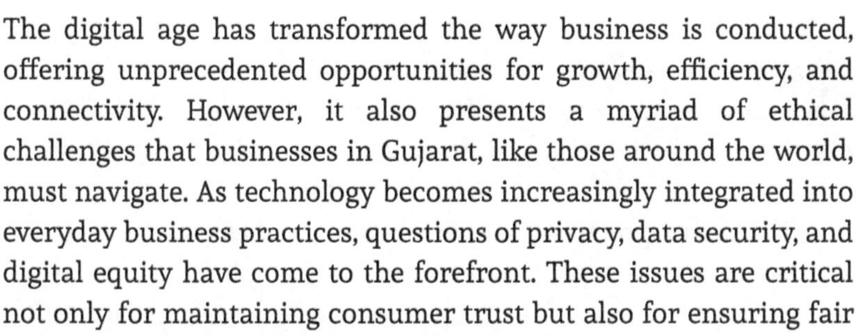

The digital age has transformed the way business is conducted, offering unprecedented opportunities for growth, efficiency, and connectivity. However, it also presents a myriad of ethical challenges that businesses in Gujarat, like those around the world, must navigate. As technology becomes increasingly integrated into everyday business practices, questions of privacy, data security, and digital equity have come to the forefront. These issues are critical not only for maintaining consumer trust but also for ensuring fair competition and protecting vulnerable populations.

Data Privacy and Security Concerns

One of the most pressing ethical challenges in the digital age is the handling of personal and sensitive data. Businesses collect vast amounts of data from customers, employees, and business partners, which can be a valuable asset when used for analysis and decision-making. However, this data is also a significant responsibility. Companies must ensure robust protections are in place to prevent data breaches, which can lead to financial loss and damage to reputation.

In Gujarat, as in many places with rapidly growing digital infrastructures, there is a continuous struggle to balance data utilization with privacy concerns. The region's businesses face the task of implementing advanced cybersecurity measures and adhering to national and international data protection regulations. Moreover, they must do so in a way that is transparent to consumers, who are increasingly aware of and concerned about privacy issues.

Transparency in the Use of Algorithms

The use of algorithms and artificial intelligence (AI) in business operations can improve efficiency and provide insights that would be impossible for humans to generate on their own. However, these technologies also raise ethical questions about transparency and accountability. Algorithms can inadvertently perpetuate biases if they are trained on biased data sets, leading to unfair or discriminatory outcomes. For example, if a hiring algorithm in Gujarat is trained on historical data that reflects past discriminatory practices, it may continue to favor certain groups over others unless explicitly corrected.

Businesses must ensure that their use of AI and algorithms is not only effective but also fair and transparent. This involves regular audits of algorithmic processes to identify and mitigate biases, as well as clear communication with stakeholders about how these technologies are used and the measures in place to ensure ethical compliance.

The Digital Divide

As digital technologies become central to business operations, the risk of the digital divide—where some individuals have fewer digital resources or skills than others—becomes more pronounced. In Gujarat, this divide can manifest in several ways, such as disparities in access to digital infrastructure between urban and rural areas or among different socioeconomic groups. The digital divide can exacerbate existing inequalities and limit opportunities for those on the wrong side of the divide.

Businesses face the ethical challenge of ensuring that their digital advancements do not leave behind a significant portion of the population. This includes investing in digital literacy programs, ensuring that services are accessible to non-digital natives, and participating in broader efforts to improve digital infrastructure. By addressing these issues, businesses can help ensure that the benefits of digital technologies are widely shared across all sections of society.

Ethical Marketing in Digital Platforms

Digital marketing offers powerful tools for businesses to reach customers, but it also introduces ethical challenges. Issues such as the manipulation of consumer behavior through data analytics, the dissemination of misleading information, and the invasion of privacy through aggressive tracking practices are areas of concern. In Gujarat, where digital marketing is becoming increasingly sophisticated, businesses must navigate these issues carefully to maintain trust and respect from consumers.

Companies need to commit to ethical marketing practices that respect consumer privacy and provide clear, truthful information. This includes obtaining consent for data collection and usage, avoiding deceptive practices, and being transparent about the use of personal data in marketing strategies.

Future Perspectives

As Gujarat continues to advance in the digital landscape, the importance of addressing these ethical challenges cannot be overstated. Companies that proactively engage with these issues not only protect themselves against risks but also build stronger relationships with stakeholders and enhance their long-term sustainability. The commitment to ethical practices in the digital age is a competitive advantage that can distinguish businesses in a crowded market.

Moreover, regulatory frameworks will likely continue to evolve in response to these challenges, and businesses in Gujarat must stay ahead of these changes by anticipating new requirements and adapting their practices accordingly. By fostering an ethical digital culture, businesses in Gujarat can lead by example, demonstrating that it is possible to achieve technological advancement without compromising on ethical standards.

ႦႦႦ

"Corporate social responsibility in Gujarat isn't just
a corporate obligation; it's a heartfelt commitment
to giving back to the communities that nurture
business success."

❥❥❥

TEN

COMMUNITY ENGAGEMENT AND CORPORATE SOCIAL RESPONSIBILITY

In Gujarat, community engagement and corporate social responsibility (CSR) are increasingly recognized as integral components of successful business strategies. As companies grow and expand their influence, their roles in their communities have evolved from mere business entities to pillars of social, economic, and environmental development. This shift reflects a broader understanding that long-term business success is deeply intertwined with the well-being of the communities they serve.

Foundations of CSR in Gujarat

The concept of CSR in Gujarat is rooted in the region's rich cultural and religious traditions, which emphasize values such as philanthropy, care for the less fortunate, and stewardship of the environment. These values are deeply embedded in the Gujarati business ethos, influencing companies to undertake initiatives that contribute positively to societal welfare.

Furthermore, India's CSR mandate, which requires companies to spend a percentage of their profits on social development, has institutionalized these practices, making Gujarat a fertile ground for innovative CSR projects. This legal framework has not only standardized the approach to CSR but has also encouraged companies to professionalize and scale their CSR activities, making them more impactful and aligned with broader developmental goals.

Integrating CSR with Business Objectives

In Gujarat, forward-thinking companies are increasingly integrating their CSR initiatives with their core business objectives. This alignment ensures that social responsibility becomes a key component of the business strategy rather than a peripheral activity. For instance, companies in the manufacturing sector often focus on environmental sustainability by reducing waste, conserving water, and lowering emissions. Similarly, tech companies might invest in improving digital literacy among underserved populations, thereby expanding their potential customer base while also contributing to social welfare.

This strategic approach to CSR not only enhances the company's reputation but also ensures that the initiatives are sustainable and generate real value both for the company and the community. By linking CSR to business outcomes, companies can justify ongoing investment in these initiatives, creating a cycle of continuous improvement and impact.

Community Engagement Practices

Community engagement in Gujarat goes beyond financial contributions, involving active participation and collaboration with local communities to identify and address their most pressing needs. Businesses often engage in dialogues with community leaders and members to understand their challenges and aspirations. This participatory approach ensures that the CSR initiatives are well-targeted and have the endorsement and support of the community, increasing their effectiveness and sustainability.

Many Gujarati companies also encourage employee volunteering, which fosters a sense of community and personal investment in the company's CSR efforts. These volunteering programs often include activities like teaching in local schools, participating in health camps, and environmental clean-ups. Such initiatives not only benefit the community but also build team spirit and morale among employees, reinforcing the company's commitment to social responsibility.

Impact on Sustainable Development

The impact of robust CSR practices in Gujarat is evident across various dimensions of sustainable development. For example, numerous companies have undertaken projects that contribute to the United Nations Sustainable Development Goals (SDGs), such as promoting quality education, ensuring clean water and sanitation, and supporting economic growth through skill development programs.

These initiatives not only address immediate community needs but also build capacities that enable long-term development. For instance, by providing vocational training and entrepreneurship development programs, companies help individuals become economically self-sufficient, which in turn stimulates local economies and reduces poverty.

Challenges and Future Directions

Despite the progress, challenges remain in ensuring that CSR efforts are as effective and impactful as possible. Issues such as project sustainability, impact measurement, and coordination among various stakeholders can hinder the success of CSR initiatives. To overcome these challenges, companies in Gujarat are increasingly adopting international best practices like impact investing and social return on investment (SROI) frameworks to measure and enhance the effectiveness of their CSR activities.

Looking ahead, the trajectory of CSR in Gujarat is likely to see even greater integration with core business practices, with a focus on innovation and partnerships. Collaborations between businesses, non-profits, government agencies, and international organizations can enhance the scale and impact of CSR initiatives, making them more transformative for the community.

Community engagement and CSR are not only about corporate benevolence but are also strategic business imperatives in today's interconnected world. In Gujarat, where business and community have always been closely linked, CSR is evolving into a sophisticated, impactful enterprise that promises to drive social and economic progress for generations to come.

ppp

"From the textile mills to the tech startups,
Gujarat's business leaders aren't just captains of
industry; they're champions of integrity, steering
their companies towards ethical excellence."

❤❤❤

ELEVEN

THE ROLE OF EDUCATION IN SHAPING ETHICAL BUSINESS LEADERS

Education plays a pivotal role in shaping the leaders of tomorrow, particularly in the business world where ethical considerations are increasingly at the forefront of organizational priorities. In Gujarat, the emphasis on education as a cornerstone for developing ethical business leaders is evident through numerous initiatives and programs that combine traditional values with modern business practices. This educational approach not only equips future leaders with the necessary skills and knowledge but also instills a deep sense of moral responsibility and ethical conduct.

Ethical Foundations in Educational Systems

In Gujarat, as in many parts of the world, the education system from the primary level onwards integrates elements of ethical training and moral development. This integration is crucial in shaping individuals' perspectives on honesty, integrity, and responsibility, long before they enter the business world. Schools and colleges in Gujarat often incorporate lessons that cover ethical dilemmas, the importance of transparency, and the impact of business on society and the environment.

Furthermore, higher education institutions in Gujarat that specialize in business and management place a strong emphasis on ethics and corporate social responsibility (CSR) as core components of their curriculum. Courses on business ethics, corporate governance, and sustainable development are common and are designed to prepare students to face the complex challenges of the modern business environment.

Case Studies and Practical Exposure

To further reinforce ethical principles, educational institutions often use case studies that present real-world scenarios requiring ethical decision-making. These case studies are an effective educational tool because they force students to consider not only the profitability of decisions but also their societal impacts. Moreover, internships and practical training opportunities allow students to experience firsthand the ethical dilemmas and challenges that occur in everyday business operations.

Gujarat's universities and business schools also facilitate interactions between students and business leaders who exemplify ethical practices in their professional lives. Guest lectures, workshops, and seminars provide platforms where experienced professionals can share their insights and experiences, which helps to underline the importance of ethics in achieving long-term business success.

Role of Governance and Compliance Training

As part of their educational journey, students in Gujarat are also taught about the importance of governance structures and compliance mechanisms in upholding ethical standards. Understanding the regulatory framework within which businesses operate helps future leaders to appreciate the necessity of compliance not just from a legal perspective but as an essential aspect of ethical business conduct. This knowledge is crucial in a world where businesses are often judged by their ability to operate transparently and with integrity.

Incorporating Technology and Ethics

With the rise of digital technologies, educational programs are increasingly focusing on the ethical aspects of technology use in business. This includes issues such as data privacy, the ethical use of artificial intelligence, and the social implications of technological disruptions. By integrating these topics into the business curriculum, educational institutions in Gujarat are preparing students to navigate the ethical landscapes of both current and future business environments.

Leadership Development and Ethical Cultures

Another critical aspect of education for ethical leadership is the development of soft skills such as empathy, communication, and teamwork. These skills are essential for creating and maintaining ethical cultures within organizations. Leadership programs designed to foster these qualities are becoming more common in Gujarat's educational institutions, emphasizing the role of leaders not only as decision-makers but also as ethical role models for their organizations.

Challenges and Opportunities

Despite the robust efforts to integrate ethics into business education, challenges remain. These include ensuring that ethical training is not just theoretical but translates into practice, and addressing the cultural and systemic pressures that might lead to unethical behavior. Additionally, as the business environment continues to evolve, educational programs must keep pace with new ethical dilemmas and scenarios.

Looking forward, the role of education in shaping ethical business leaders in Gujarat is expected to grow even more significant. As global business challenges become more complex and intertwined with social and environmental issues, the demand for leaders who can navigate these challenges ethically and effectively will continue to rise. Gujarat's educational institutions are well-positioned to meet this demand, continuing to innovate and adapt their curricula to develop leaders who can not only succeed in business but also contribute positively to society.

$$\triangleright\triangleright\triangleright$$

"In Gujarat, success isn't measured just by profits;
it's defined by the positive impact businesses have
on society and the environment."

ᗞᗞᗞ

TWELVE

INTERSECTING BUSINESS WITH GUJARAT'S ART AND CULTURE

The intersection of business with Gujarat's rich art and culture is a dynamic space where traditional practices meet modern entrepreneurship. This fusion not only preserves and promotes Gujarati culture but also creates substantial economic opportunities by turning cultural assets into marketable products and experiences. As businesses in Gujarat leverage the state's cultural heritage, they contribute to a vibrant cultural economy that attracts tourism, fosters community pride, and opens up new avenues for innovation.

Cultural Heritage as a Business Asset

Gujarat is home to a diverse array of cultural and artistic traditions, from the textile arts of Kutch embroidery and Patola weaving to the performing arts such as Garba and Bhavai. These traditions are not only expressions of cultural identity but also significant economic resources. Recognizing this, businesses in Gujarat have developed models to harness these cultural assets, turning them into products and services that appeal to both local and global markets.

One successful model is the collaboration between artisans and modern businesses to create high-quality, culturally infused products that meet contemporary aesthetic standards while remaining true to traditional craftsmanship. This approach not only helps preserve the unique crafts of Gujarat but also ensures a sustainable income for artisans, who are often challenged by the economic viability of their traditional practices.

Enhancing Global Appeal

Gujarati businesses have also been instrumental in marketing their cultural products on a global scale. By participating in international trade shows, online marketplaces, and cultural festivals, they introduce Gujarat's arts and crafts to the world, thereby expanding their markets and enhancing the cultural profile of the state. This global exposure not only boosts the economy but also fosters cultural exchange and appreciation, establishing Gujarat as a hub of vibrant cultural tourism.

The film industry in Gujarat is another area where culture intersects with business. Gujarati cinema, with its focus on regional stories and traditions, has seen a resurgence in popularity. This revival is supported by investments from local businesses that see value in promoting Gujarati language and culture through cinema. The success of these films in domestic and diaspora markets underscores the potential of cultural industries to drive business growth and cultural preservation.

Cultural Tourism and Economic Development

Cultural tourism is a significant aspect of how business intersects with art and culture in Gujarat. The state's numerous festivals, historical sites, and artisan villages are not just tourist attractions but also part of a broader strategy to promote economic development through culture. Businesses invest in developing infrastructure, services, and marketing strategies that enhance the visitor experience while respecting and preserving the cultural integrity of the attractions.

Hotels, travel agencies, and event companies collaborate with cultural institutions and communities to create immersive experiences for tourists. These range from heritage walks and craft workshops to cultural performances and culinary tours, all designed to deepen visitors' understanding of Gujarati culture while generating revenue for local businesses and communities.

Innovation in Cultural Enterprises

Innovation is key to merging business with culture in ways that are sustainable and relevant in the modern world. For example, digital technology is being employed to archive cultural practices and promote them through various media. Virtual reality experiences that showcase Gujarat's cultural sites, online platforms that sell traditional arts and crafts, and digital marketing strategies targeting niche audiences are all examples of how businesses are innovatively promoting culture.

Moreover, educational initiatives that focus on teaching the business skills necessary to manage cultural enterprises are emerging. These programs, often developed in partnership with universities and business schools, help cultivate a new generation of entrepreneurs who are well-versed in both business and cultural management.

Challenges and Opportunities

Despite the successful integration of business and culture, challenges remain. Balancing commercial interests with the authenticity and preservation of cultural heritage requires careful management. There is also the risk of cultural commodification, where the cultural elements are detached from their original context and meaning.

To address these challenges, businesses and cultural leaders in Gujarat are increasingly focusing on ethical practices and sustainable models that prioritize community involvement and benefits. By ensuring that the communities which uphold these cultural traditions are active participants in and beneficiaries of the cultural economy, Gujarat can set an example of how to integrate business with culture in a way that is respectful, sustainable, and economically beneficial.

The intersection of business with art and culture in Gujarat represents a fertile ground for economic and cultural flourishing. As Gujarat continues to innovate within this space, it not only preserves its rich cultural heritage but also transforms it into a key driver of its modern economy. This approach not only enhances the cultural fabric of the state but also sets a benchmark for how regions around the world can integrate culture and business to mutual benefit.

ᐳᐳᐳ

"The future of business in Gujarat isn't just about expansion; it's about evolution, where traditional values meet modern challenges with innovative solutions."

❦❦❦

THIRTEEN

NAVIGATING GLOBAL MARKETS WITH LOCAL VALUES

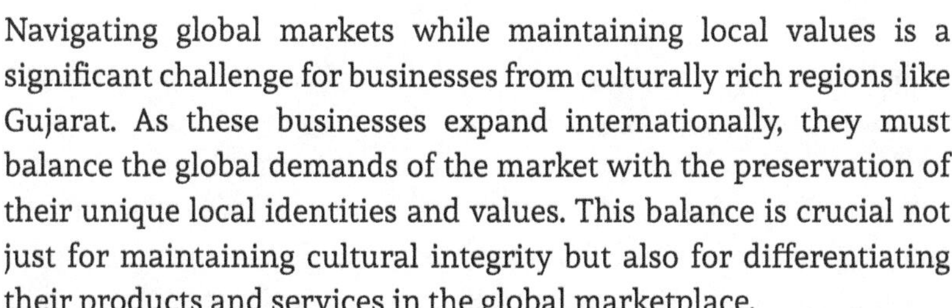

Navigating global markets while maintaining local values is a significant challenge for businesses from culturally rich regions like Gujarat. As these businesses expand internationally, they must balance the global demands of the market with the preservation of their unique local identities and values. This balance is crucial not just for maintaining cultural integrity but also for differentiating their products and services in the global marketplace.

Understanding Global Market Dynamics

The first step for any business looking to expand into global markets is to understand the diverse dynamics of these markets. This involves studying not only the economic and regulatory landscapes but also the cultural nuances that influence consumer behavior. For Gujarati businesses, which are deeply rooted in the traditions and values of their local culture, this understanding is critical to ensure that they can effectively communicate the value of their culturally-infused products or services.

Gujarati businesses have historically excelled in industries such as textiles, diamonds, and agriculture, leveraging their local expertise on a global scale. The challenge, however, is to adapt these products to different cultural contexts without diluting the core values that define their uniqueness.

Balancing Local Values with Global Practices

One of the most significant aspects of navigating global markets is the ability to balance local values with the need to adapt to global business practices. For instance, businesses from Gujarat are often family-owned, with strong values around community, respect, and ethical behavior. When these businesses enter more competitive international markets, they must find ways to maintain these values in the face of diverse business practices and ethical standards.

This balance can be achieved by embedding local values into the business strategy, such as by implementing fair trade practices, ensuring ethical labor practices, and committing to environmental sustainability. These values not only help maintain the cultural integrity of the business but also appeal to global consumers who are increasingly concerned about the ethical aspects of their purchases.

Leveraging Cultural Heritage for Market Differentiation

Gujarati businesses can use their rich cultural heritage as a differentiator in the global market. Products such as Gujarati handicrafts, textiles, and jewelry carry with them stories and traditions that can be marketed as unique selling propositions. By emphasizing the craftsmanship, history, and cultural significance of their products, businesses can create a niche market that values authenticity and cultural richness.

Moreover, storytelling can be a powerful tool in marketing these products. By sharing the stories behind their products, businesses not only educate their consumers about the cultural context but also create emotional connections that can drive loyalty and appreciation.

Strategies for Global Expansion

Strategic partnerships and collaborations with foreign companies can also facilitate smoother entry into global markets while preserving local values. These partnerships can help navigate the regulatory and logistical challenges of international business. Additionally, they can provide local businesses with insights into consumer behavior and market trends in different regions, which can be invaluable in tailoring products and marketing strategies to suit global tastes.

Furthermore, attending international trade fairs and cultural exhibitions can help businesses showcase their products and reach a wider audience. These events provide a platform for cultural exchange and open up opportunities for exporting local products to foreign markets.

Challenges and Opportunities

The journey of taking local values to global markets is fraught with challenges. There is always the risk of losing the essence of what makes these businesses unique as they scale and adapt to new markets. Moreover, global competition demands constant innovation and adaptation, which can strain resources and divert focus from traditional practices.

However, the opportunities presented by global markets are immense. By successfully navigating these markets, businesses can achieve substantial growth and bring about greater economic prosperity not just for themselves but also for the communities they represent. This success, in turn, can inspire other local businesses to venture into global markets, fostering a culture of innovation and global thinking.

As businesses from Gujarat navigate global markets, they carry with them the profound responsibility of balancing economic goals with the preservation of their local values. By effectively managing this balance, they not only ensure their own sustainability but also contribute to the global appreciation of Gujarat's rich cultural heritage. This approach not only helps in achieving business success but also in making a significant impact on the global cultural economy.

ᕐᕐᕐ

"Gujarat's business culture isn't just about competition; it's about collaboration, where companies work together to achieve shared goals and drive collective prosperity."

❦❦❦

FOURTEEN

YOUTH ENTREPRENEURSHIP: ETHICS AND ASPIRATIONS

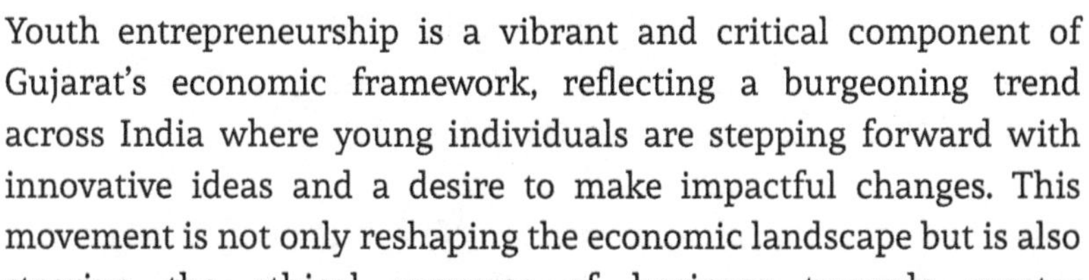

Youth entrepreneurship is a vibrant and critical component of Gujarat's economic framework, reflecting a burgeoning trend across India where young individuals are stepping forward with innovative ideas and a desire to make impactful changes. This movement is not only reshaping the economic landscape but is also steering the ethical compass of business towards greater transparency, responsibility, and community-oriented growth.

The Rise of Youth Entrepreneurship

In recent years, Gujarat has seen a significant rise in youth entrepreneurship, driven by an increasingly supportive ecosystem that includes easier access to capital, mentorship programs, and governmental support. Universities and educational institutions across the state are fostering this trend by integrating entrepreneurship training into their curricula and establishing incubators to help students transform their ideas into viable businesses.

Young entrepreneurs in Gujarat are characterized by their dynamism and willingness to take risks. They are more likely to venture into new, unexplored sectors such as technology, renewable energy, and e-commerce. These sectors not only promise substantial economic returns but also offer the potential to address pressing global issues like sustainability, energy conservation, and digital inclusion.

Embedding Ethics in Entrepreneurial Ventures

Ethics play a crucial role in the new wave of entrepreneurial ventures led by the youth. Young entrepreneurs are increasingly aware of the social and environmental impacts of their businesses and strive to build enterprises that are not only profitable but also ethically sound and socially responsible. This ethical sensitivity reflects a broader shift in global business practices towards sustainability and corporate social responsibility.

One of the key ethical considerations for young entrepreneurs in Gujarat is the commitment to fair labor practices. Many startups are taking proactive steps to ensure their operations are free from exploitation and that they provide fair wages and safe working conditions. This commitment is often rooted in the personal values of the founders, many of whom are motivated by a desire to improve their communities and society at large.

Challenges Facing Young Entrepreneurs

Despite the supportive ecosystem, young entrepreneurs in Gujarat face several challenges. Access to funding remains a significant hurdle, with many young founders lacking the collateral or track record to secure loans from traditional financial institutions. While venture capital and angel investing are growing, these sources of funding are highly competitive and not accessible to all.

Additionally, navigating the regulatory environment can be daunting for young entrepreneurs. The bureaucracy involved in setting up and running a business can be cumbersome and time-consuming. Young entrepreneurs must be adept not only at managing their business but also at understanding and complying with various laws and regulations.

The Role of Technology and Innovation

Technology plays a pivotal role in the businesses of young entrepreneurs. Many youth-led startups are based on new technologies or innovative uses of existing technologies. From mobile applications that improve healthcare accessibility to platforms that connect artisans with global markets, technology enables these young businesses to scale rapidly and impact widely.

Moreover, innovation is not limited to product development or technology use. It also extends to business models. Young entrepreneurs in Gujarat are experimenting with models such as social enterprises, which combine profit-making with social impact, and cooperative models, which focus on stakeholder engagement and community benefits.

Aspirations and Future Directions

The aspirations of young entrepreneurs in Gujarat extend beyond financial success. Many are driven by a vision to contribute to their communities and to build businesses that reflect their ethical beliefs and values. This generation of entrepreneurs is not only looking to change the economic fabric of Gujarat but also to influence societal norms and practices towards greater equity and sustainability.

Looking forward, the trajectory for youth entrepreneurship in Gujarat is overwhelmingly positive. Continued support from the government and private sectors, coupled with a robust educational foundation in entrepreneurship, promises to sustain and amplify this trend. Moreover, as global issues increasingly demand innovative solutions, the creativity and ethical commitment of Gujarat's young entrepreneurs position them well to lead these efforts.

Youth entrepreneurship in Gujarat is a powerful force for economic and social change. By embedding ethics and aspirations in their business practices, young entrepreneurs are setting new standards for what it means to be successful in business. Their efforts are not only creating wealth but also advancing the well-being of their communities and the broader society, marking a new chapter in Gujarat's entrepreneurial story.

♭♭♭

"Entrepreneurship in Gujarat isn't just about individual ambition; it's about community empowerment, where startups create jobs, foster innovation, and uplift society."

❦❦❦

FIFTEEN

TRANSPARENCY IN THE DIAMOND INDUSTRY: A CASE STUDY

The diamond industry, particularly in Gujarat, has long been one of the economic backbones of the region, with Surat famously known as the diamond hub of the world. However, the industry has also faced its fair share of challenges, especially regarding transparency and ethical practices. The journey towards transparency in this lucrative sector offers valuable insights into how businesses can evolve to meet higher ethical standards and consumer expectations in a globalized market.

Historical Context and Challenges

Historically, the diamond industry in Gujarat has operated within a somewhat opaque framework, where transactions were often conducted based on trust and verbal agreements without much formal documentation. While this system worked for many years, it presented significant challenges, such as the risk of fraud, smuggling, and the sale of conflict diamonds, which fueled wars and human rights abuses in parts of Africa.

The lack of transparency also made it difficult for consumers to trust the provenance and quality of diamonds. With growing global awareness about the source of diamonds and the conditions under which they were mined and processed, consumers began to demand more accountability from the industry.

Initiatives for Enhancing Transparency

Recognizing the need for change, stakeholders within Gujarat's diamond industry, including traders, manufacturers, and government bodies, began implementing several initiatives aimed at enhancing transparency. One of the most significant steps was the adoption of the Kimberley Process Certification Scheme (KPCS). The KPCS is an international system that aims to prevent "conflict diamonds" from entering the mainstream rough diamond market. It requires that each shipment of rough diamonds across international borders be certified by a government-validated Kimberley Process certificate stating that the diamonds are conflict-free.

In addition to adhering to international standards like the KPCS, many businesses in the diamond industry have started investing in technology to improve traceability. Blockchain technology, for instance, has been increasingly adopted as it offers a way to track the journey of a diamond from the mine to the market in an immutable ledger, ensuring that the data cannot be altered retroactively.

Case Studies of Successful Implementation

A notable example of successful transparency enhancement in Gujarat's diamond industry is seen in the operations of some of

Surat's largest diamond processing firms. These firms have integrated comprehensive traceability technologies that not only ensure compliance with the Kimberley Process but also provide consumers with detailed histories of their purchased diamonds. This information includes the diamond's origin, the conditions under which it was mined, cut, and polished, and its journey through the supply chain.

These firms also engage in regular audits and third-party verifications to ensure that their practices remain transparent and up to standard. Such measures have not only improved consumer trust but also enhanced the global reputation of Gujarat's diamond industry.

Impact on the Industry and Stakeholders

The move towards greater transparency has had a profound impact on the diamond industry in Gujarat. It has opened up new markets, particularly in Western countries where consumers are highly sensitive to ethical considerations. Transparency has also led to better labor practices and improved working conditions in the mines and factories, as these aspects are now closely monitored and reported.

Furthermore, transparency initiatives have helped protect the industry from fluctuations in global markets. Consumers are more willing to invest in diamonds that are certified to be ethically sourced, providing a competitive edge to businesses that can prove the integrity of their supply chains.

Future Prospects and Continuing Challenges

While significant progress has been made, the journey towards full transparency is ongoing. Challenges remain, such as ensuring that all players in the industry, especially the smaller firms and individual traders, comply with the established standards. There is also the challenge of continuously updating and securing technology platforms to keep up with global advancements and potential cybersecurity threats.

Looking forward, the diamond industry in Gujarat is well-positioned to lead by example in transparency and ethical practices. Continued commitment to these ideals, coupled with the adoption of advanced technologies and robust regulatory frameworks, will be crucial for sustaining and building on the gains made so far.

The case study of the diamond industry in Gujarat illustrates the complex yet rewarding path toward transparency in a traditionally opaque sector. It highlights the critical role of technology, international cooperation, and consumer-driven demand in shaping industry practices. As the industry continues to evolve, the lessons learned from Gujarat's experience can offer valuable insights for other sectors striving to enhance transparency and ethical practices in their operations.

ϷϷϷ

"Gujarat's commitment to ethical business practices
isn't just a trend; it's a timeless tradition rooted in
the state's rich cultural heritage."

ᐳᐳᐳ

SIXTEEN

THE IMPACT OF RELIGIOUS AND SPIRITUAL VALUES IN BUSINESS

In Gujarat, the intersection of religious and spiritual values with business practices is a defining characteristic of the region's commercial landscape. These values, deeply rooted in the local culture, significantly influence how businesses operate, guiding everything from management styles to corporate missions and interactions with stakeholders. The role of religion and spirituality in business is not merely a backdrop but an active and dynamic part of daily business operations, shaping the ethical frameworks and contributing to the overall success and sustainability of enterprises.

Religious and Spiritual Foundations in Gujarati Business

Gujarat is a melting pot of various religions, including Hinduism, Jainism, Islam, and others, each contributing uniquely to the business ethos of the region. For instance, Jainism, which emphasizes principles such as non-violence (ahimsa), honesty (satya), and non-possessiveness (aparigraha), heavily influences the diamond and textile industries, where Jains hold significant stakes. These principles encourage businesses to adopt fair practices, avoid exploitation, and engage in philanthropy.

Similarly, Hindu philosophies like 'Karma' (actions) and 'Dharma' (duty/righteousness) play crucial roles in shaping business practices. These concepts teach that one's actions, including in business, should adhere to moral values and that each individual has a duty to perform their role with integrity and fairness.

Ethical Business Practices

The impact of these religious and spiritual values is most visibly reflected in the ethical practices that many Gujarati businesses adhere to. This includes fair treatment of employees, ethical sourcing and selling practices, and a strong emphasis on community welfare and development. Many businesses in Gujarat are family-owned and have been for generations, and these values are passed down and remain intact over the years, reinforcing a culture of ethical business practices.

Moreover, many companies engage in CSR activities not just for compliance but as a fundamental aspect of their business philosophy influenced by their religious and spiritual beliefs. These activities often focus on areas such as education, healthcare, and community development, reflecting the values of service and charity that are emphasized in many religious teachings.

Trust and Reputation in Business

Trust and reputation are critical in business, and in Gujarat, where much of business historically relied on word-of-mouth and personal relationships, religious and spiritual integrity are key assets. For instance, the concept of 'Vishwas' (trust) in business dealings is highly regarded, with many deals still being made on the basis of trust without extensive legal documentation. This practice not only speeds up transactions but also builds long-term business relationships that stand the test of time.

Challenges of Modernization and Globalization

As Gujarati businesses expand globally, they encounter diverse business environments and cultures that sometimes challenge their traditional value systems. Navigating these challenges while maintaining their core values is a delicate balance. For example, global markets often demand rapid scalability and competitiveness that can pressure businesses to compromise on their ethical standards. However, many Gujarati businesses have turned this challenge into an opportunity by using their commitment to ethical practices and community-oriented business models as unique selling points in the global marketplace.

The Role of Spirituality in Leadership and Innovation

Spirituality also plays a role in leadership and innovation within Gujarati businesses. Spiritual practices such as meditation and yoga are increasingly being incorporated into the business environment to enhance decision-making capabilities, reduce stress, and improve overall well-being. These practices are believed to foster a clearer understanding of one's roles and responsibilities and encourage a more compassionate approach to management and labor relations.

Moreover, the spiritual approach often leads to more sustainable and innovative business practices. For instance, the concept of 'Seva' (selfless service) drives many entrepreneurs to innovate in areas that contribute to societal welfare, such as renewable energy, sustainable agriculture, and healthcare.

Sustaining Traditional Values in a Changing World

Preserving traditional religious and spiritual values in a rapidly modernizing world is an ongoing challenge for Gujarati businesses. However, these values provide a strong foundation and guiding principles that help businesses adapt without losing their identity. Education and continuous learning about the importance of these values in business schools and through mentorship programs help perpetuate these ideals.

The impact of religious and spiritual values on business in Gujarat is profound and multifaceted, influencing ethical practices, leadership styles, and community engagement. These values not only enrich the business culture but also enhance competitiveness and sustainability, providing a robust model for integrating deep-seated cultural values with modern business practices. As Gujarat continues to be a significant player on the global stage, the role of these spiritual and religious values will undoubtedly continue to shape its business practices and innovations.

"From the boardroom to the factory floor, Gujarat's business leaders aren't just influencers; they're visionaries, shaping the future with integrity and foresight."

❧❧❧

SEVENTEEN

INNOVATIONS IN AGRICULTURE: ETHICAL PRACTICES AND TECHNIQUES

In Gujarat, a region known for its agricultural innovation and rich farming heritage, the integration of ethical practices and advanced techniques into agriculture is reshaping the industry. This integration is crucial for sustainable growth and environmental sustainability, reflecting a broader shift in global agricultural practices toward more responsible farming. In Gujarat, these innovations are not just enhancing productivity and profitability but are also ensuring the welfare of the community and the preservation of the ecosystem.

Sustainable Farming Techniques

One of the core areas of innovation in Gujarat's agriculture is the adoption of sustainable farming techniques. These techniques are designed to minimize environmental impact, conserve water, and reduce chemical inputs, all while maintaining or increasing farm productivity. Techniques such as drip irrigation, which dramatically reduces water usage compared to traditional flood irrigation, have been widely adopted in Gujarat. Drip irrigation not only conserves water but also ensures that water is delivered directly to the plant roots, reducing evaporation and runoff.

Another significant innovation has been the use of organic farming practices. Many farmers in Gujarat have turned to organic agriculture to produce crops free from chemical pesticides and fertilizers. This shift not only appeals to the growing global demand for organic products but also promotes soil health and biodiversity. Organic farming in Gujarat has been supported by both government initiatives and private enterprises, which provide farmers with the training and resources needed to transition from conventional methods.

Precision Agriculture

The adoption of precision agriculture technologies is another area where Gujarat is leading by example. Precision agriculture involves the use of GPS technology, drones, IoT devices, and big data analytics to monitor and optimize the growth conditions of crops. For instance, drones are used for aerial surveys of large farms to assess crop health, monitor irrigation systems, and even perform tasks like seeding and spraying. This high-tech approach allows farmers to make informed decisions that enhance productivity and reduce waste.

Ethical Labor Practices

Ethical labor practices are a significant concern in the agricultural sector, where labor rights abuses and child labor have historically been problems. In Gujarat, more and more agricultural businesses are committing to ethical labor practices by ensuring fair wages, safe working conditions, and regular working hours for farmworkers. These practices are not only ethically important but also contribute to better labor relations and higher productivity, as well-motivated workers are likely to be more efficient.

Community Involvement and Education

Community involvement is integral to the sustainable development of agriculture in Gujarat. Many innovative projects involve local communities in the planning and implementation stages, which helps ensure that the projects are well-adapted to local needs and conditions. Moreover, education plays a critical role in spreading innovative and ethical agricultural practices. Educational programs aimed at farmers often include training on sustainable farming techniques, the use of technology in agriculture, and the importance of ethical labor practices.

Crop Diversification and Resilience

Crop diversification is another area where Gujarat is seeing a lot of innovative activity. By diversifying the types of crops grown, farmers can reduce dependency on a single crop, thus spreading risk and increasing resilience against crop failures. Diversification also helps in maintaining soil fertility and combating pests and diseases naturally. Moreover, it aligns with ethical practices by promoting a more balanced ecosystem.

Challenges and Future Directions

Despite these innovations, the agricultural sector in Gujarat faces ongoing challenges. Climate change poses a significant risk, with increasing temperatures and changing rainfall patterns affecting crop yields. Additionally, the small size of many farms in Gujarat can make it difficult for farmers to invest in expensive new technologies or implement large-scale changes.

However, the future looks promising as continued technological advancements and governmental support are likely to further empower farmers. Innovations such as gene editing and advanced biotechnologies are on the horizon, offering potential solutions to some of the most pressing agricultural challenges.

The innovations in agriculture in Gujarat demonstrate how integrating ethical practices with advanced techniques can lead to a more sustainable and productive agricultural sector. These innovations not only contribute to economic growth but also ensure environmental sustainability and social welfare, creating a model for responsible agriculture that can be replicated globally. As Gujarat continues to innovate in this area, it stands as a beacon of how agriculture can evolve to meet the needs of both the present and the future, responsibly and sustainably.

ppp

"In Gujarat, ethical leadership isn't just a choice;
it's a responsibility, where business decisions are
guided by principles of honesty, fairness, and
accountability."

❥❥❥

EIGHTEEN

Responsible Tourism in Gujarat

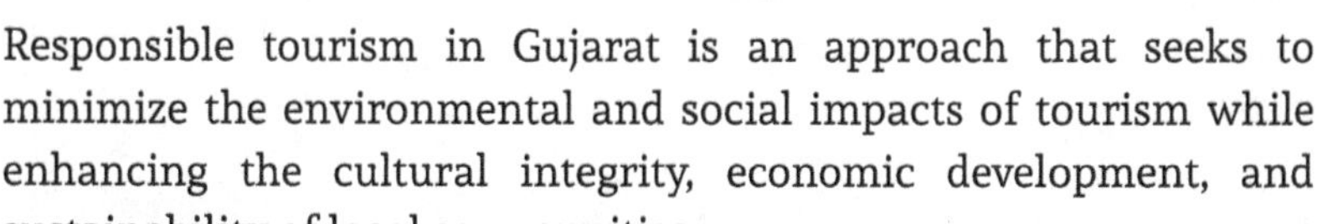

Responsible tourism in Gujarat is an approach that seeks to minimize the environmental and social impacts of tourism while enhancing the cultural integrity, economic development, and sustainability of local communities.

This model of tourism is particularly significant in Gujarat, a state rich in cultural heritage, natural landscapes, and historical sites, where the influx of tourists can have profound impacts on the local ecosystem and its inhabitants.

Principles of Responsible Tourism

Responsible tourism in Gujarat is grounded in several key principles: environmental integrity, social justice, economic benefit to local communities, and cultural respect. The aim is to create a positive experience for both visitors and hosts, providing meaningful connections with local people, and promoting greater understanding of local cultural, social, and environmental issues.

Sustainable Practices in Tourism Development

Gujarat's approach to responsible tourism includes sustainable practices that are designed to preserve the region's natural resources while accommodating tourists.

For example, many of Gujarat's wildlife sanctuaries and national parks, such as Gir National Park, home to the Asiatic lion, implement strict guidelines on the number of visitors and the type of activities allowed to minimize human impact on wildlife and habitats.

Eco-friendly accommodations are another facet of sustainable tourism that Gujarat is embracing. These facilities are designed to be energy-efficient, often using solar power, and minimize waste through recycling and composting. They also use water-saving devices to conserve water, a critical resource in Gujarat's arid climate.

Empowering Local Communities

A central aspect of responsible tourism in Gujarat is the empowerment of local communities. This empowerment comes through ensuring that tourism provides economic benefits to the communities.

Local people are involved in the tourism industry through employment opportunities, and the benefits are shared widely, reducing income inequality. Moreover, tourism initiatives often support local artisans by providing platforms to showcase and sell their handicrafts, such as the famous Kutch embroidery and Patola silk weaving.

Training programs are also provided to locals to develop skills related to the tourism industry, including language skills, hospitality management, and guide training. These programs help elevate the standard of services offered and ensure that tourists have enriching experiences guided by knowledgeable locals.

Cultural Sensitivity and Integrity

Maintaining cultural sensitivity and integrity is paramount in Gujarat's tourism model. Efforts are made to educate tourists about local customs, traditions, and etiquette to foster respect and understanding. Tourist guides play a crucial role in this educational aspect, providing insights into the cultural significance of the sites visited and the local customs and lifestyles.

Cultural tours and heritage walks are popular in cities like Ahmedabad, which was declared a UNESCO World Heritage City. These tours are carefully designed to respect the historic and cultural significance of the locations while allowing tourists to experience Gujarat's rich history and architecture firsthand.

Challenges and Strategies for Sustainable Growth

Despite the advances in responsible tourism, challenges remain. These include managing the balance between increasing tourist numbers and preserving natural and cultural resources, dealing with the waste generated by tourism, and ensuring that tourism development does not lead to cultural homogenization.

To address these challenges, the government of Gujarat and various NGOs are implementing strategies to manage tourist flows to sensitive areas, developing more stringent regulations around waste management, and promoting less visited sites to distribute tourist numbers more evenly across the state.

Future Prospects

Looking forward, Gujarat aims to be a leader in responsible tourism in India. This vision involves not only expanding current initiatives but also continuously seeking innovative ways to enhance the sustainability of tourism practices.

The focus is on integrating new technologies for better resource management, enhancing visitor experiences through virtual and augmented reality, and increasing global awareness of Gujarat as a destination that offers both cultural richness and commitment to sustainability.

Responsible tourism in Gujarat is about creating a sustainable and inclusive approach that benefits both the state and its visitors.

By focusing on environmental conservation, social responsibility, economic benefits for local communities, and cultural integrity, Gujarat sets a compelling example of how tourism can be transformed into a force for good, promoting not just travel but also mutual respect and sustainable development.

"The success of Gujarat's businesses isn't just measured by market share; it's defined by the trust and respect they earn from customers, employees, and stakeholders."

❦❦❦

NINETEEN

FUTURE TRENDS IN ETHICAL BUSINESS PRACTICES

As businesses around the world continue to evolve under the increasing scrutiny of consumers, stakeholders, and regulators, the emphasis on ethical practices has become more pronounced. Gujarat, with its rich business heritage and burgeoning economy, is no exception to this trend. Future trends in ethical business practices are expected to shape the way companies operate, focusing on transparency, sustainability, social responsibility, and technological integration.

Enhanced Transparency and Accountability

One of the primary trends in ethical business practices is the increasing demand for transparency and accountability. Consumers and investors are more informed and concerned than ever about how companies conduct their business. This trend is driving businesses to be more open about their operations, supply chains, and financial dealings. In Gujarat, where industries such as textiles and diamonds are significant to the economy, companies are adopting technologies like blockchain to ensure product traceability and authenticity. Such technologies can record every step of a product's journey, from production to sale, ensuring that all claims about ethical sourcing and sustainability can be verified independently.

Greater Focus on Sustainability

Sustainability has transitioned from a niche concern to a central business strategy. Companies in Gujarat are increasingly integrating sustainability into their core business operations rather than treating it as an external concern. This includes adopting renewable energy sources, minimizing waste, and using environmentally friendly materials. For instance, the burgeoning solar power industry in Gujarat not only helps companies reduce their carbon footprint but also positions them as leaders in renewable energy adoption. Similarly, industries are investing in sustainable water management practices, crucial in Gujarat's largely arid environment, to ensure they use water resources judiciously.

Corporate Social Responsibility as a Business Imperative

Corporate social responsibility (CSR) is set to evolve from a mere compliance requirement to a critical component of business strategy. In Gujarat, businesses are expected to ramp up their CSR efforts, focusing not just on charity but on creating tangible impacts in areas such as education, healthcare, and community development. This shift is partly driven by regulatory requirements but also by the recognition that sustainable community relations are essential for long-term business success. Companies are finding that robust CSR programs can enhance their reputations, attract better talent, and open up new markets.

Ethical AI and Data Usage

As businesses in Gujarat increasingly rely on digital technologies and data analytics, the ethical use of artificial intelligence (AI) and data has become a critical concern. With AI being used for everything from customer service to supply chain management, ensuring these systems are unbiased and transparent is crucial. Businesses are expected to implement more stringent data governance frameworks and adopt principles of ethical AI, which include transparency, justice and fairness, non-malfeasance, responsibility, and privacy.

Employee Well-being and Inclusive Workplaces

The future of ethical business practices also includes a stronger focus on employee well-being and the creation of inclusive workplaces. This trend is partly driven by the younger workforce, who prioritize the ethical stance and workplace culture of their employers. Companies in Gujarat are increasingly adopting policies that support work-life balance, provide fair and equal opportunities, and foster a workplace culture that is free from discrimination. This not only helps in attracting and retaining talent but also boosts productivity and employee satisfaction.

Challenges and Opportunities

Despite these positive trends, challenges remain. These include resistance to change in traditional business sectors, the high cost of implementing new technologies, and the complexity of global supply chains. However, the opportunities outweigh the challenges, as ethical business practices open up new markets and build customer loyalty. Companies that are early adopters of these trends can differentiate themselves and establish leadership in their industries.

Looking Ahead

The landscape of ethical business practices is dynamic and requires continuous adaptation and innovation. Companies in Gujarat that anticipate and respond to these trends not only enhance their competitiveness but also contribute to the sustainable development of the region. As global expectations around corporate behavior continue to evolve, embracing these trends is not just beneficial but essential for businesses aiming to succeed in the modern marketplace.

The future trends in ethical business practices are set to redefine the traditional business models in Gujarat, steering them towards greater transparency, accountability, and social responsibility. These changes will not only foster a healthier business environment but also contribute to the overall socio-economic welfare of the broader community.

❦❦❦

"Gujarat's journey to global leadership isn't just about economic growth; it's about sustainable development, where prosperity is shared equitably and responsibly."

❧❧❧

TWENTY

Reflections and Moving Forward: Gujarat's Path to Global Leadership

Gujarat's journey towards global leadership in various sectors is a compelling narrative of transformation and strategic foresight. The state's trajectory from a regionally important market to a significant player on the global stage is underpinned by a blend of robust economic policies, entrepreneurial spirit, and a commitment to sustainable and ethical practices. As Gujarat continues to grow and evolve, reflections on its past successes and challenges, coupled with a forward-looking strategy, are crucial for shaping its future.

Leveraging Geographic and Cultural Advantages

Gujarat's geographical location on the western coast of India provides it with strategic access to various international trade routes. This advantage has historically facilitated the state's prominence in trade and commerce, particularly in sectors like textiles, diamonds, and petrochemicals. To build on this natural advantage, Gujarat has invested heavily in developing world-class ports and transport infrastructure, which are critical components in its path to becoming a global trading hub.

Culturally, Gujarat's diverse and entrepreneurial community has played a pivotal role in its economic success. The state's business culture, enriched by a mix of traditional values and modern practices, fosters innovation and agility—qualities that are imperative in the global market. Moving forward, nurturing this culture through education and continuous learning will be vital in maintaining Gujarat's competitive edge.

Strengthening Economic Foundations

The economic landscape of Gujarat is marked by a diversified industrial base, with strong sectors like manufacturing, agriculture, and services. The state government has played a significant role in this diversification through policies that encourage investment and innovation. Special economic zones (SEZs) and business-friendly regulatory environments have attracted both domestic and international investors.

However, for sustained growth and to avoid economic stagnation, Gujarat must continue to innovate and adapt to changing global economic conditions. This includes investing in new technologies, especially in areas like renewable energy, information technology, and biotechnology, which are expected to dominate the future global economy.

Commitment to Sustainable Development

Sustainability is a critical component of Gujarat's vision for the future. The state has made significant strides in integrating sustainable practices into its development plans. Initiatives such as the Jyotigram Yojana, which ensured reliable electricity supply to rural areas, and investments in solar energy are examples of Gujarat's commitment to sustainable growth.

Expanding these initiatives to include broader environmental concerns such as water conservation, waste management, and biodiversity preservation will be essential. As Gujarat aims for global leadership, adopting a green economy will not only enhance its environmental standing but also attract green finance and investments, which are increasingly becoming a priority for global investors.

Enhancing Social Equity and Quality of Life

Economic growth must be inclusive to be sustainable. Gujarat's path forward includes addressing social equity issues such as education, healthcare, and gender equality. Improving access to quality education and healthcare ensures that all sections of society can participate in and benefit from the state's economic growth. Moreover, empowering women and other marginalized groups through targeted programs will help unleash the full potential of Gujarat's human resources.

Embracing Globalization and International Collaboration

Gujarat's path to global leadership involves not only internal development but also active engagement with the global community. This includes fostering trade relationships, attracting foreign direct investment, and participating in international dialogues on trade, climate change, and technology.

Additionally, Gujarat can enhance its global leadership by exporting its models of success in areas like renewable energy and urban planning. Sharing its experiences and learning from others through international collaborations can elevate its status on the world stage.

Looking to the Future

As Gujarat reflects on its past achievements and challenges, the path forward requires a balanced approach that considers economic, environmental, and social dimensions. Strategic planning and execution, coupled with a willingness to innovate and adapt, will be crucial in overcoming future challenges and seizing opportunities.

Gujarat's journey towards global leadership is an ongoing process of transformation and growth. By leveraging its strengths, addressing its challenges, and embracing a sustainable and inclusive development model, Gujarat can achieve its aspiration to not only lead on a national level but also make a significant impact globally.

ppp

"In Gujarat, business isn't just about transactions; it's about relationships, built on trust, transparency, and a shared commitment to ethical excellence."

ᗄᗄᗄ

TWENTY-ONE
SUMMARY

As we traverse the diverse and vibrant business landscape of Gujarat, it becomes evident that the region is not just an economic powerhouse but also a beacon of ethical business practices and cultural richness. This exploration delves deep into the various facets of Gujarat's business culture, shedding light on how traditional values intertwine with modern entrepreneurial spirit to create a unique business environment that is both competitive and sustainable.

The foundation of Gujarat's business ethos is deeply rooted in its rich history and diverse cultural heritage. The state's strategic position along ancient trade routes has historically made it a melting pot of cultural and commercial activities. This has cultivated a business acumen characterized by an inherent trust and a knack for trade, which have evolved over centuries. Today, Gujarat stands as a testament to how traditional values can seamlessly integrate with global business practices to foster environments that are not just economically prosperous but also socially responsible and environmentally conscious.

Key to understanding Gujarat's business model is the emphasis on family and community. Many of Gujarat's businesses are family-owned, where leadership and ethics are passed down through generations, ensuring that the core values of trust, respect, and community service remain intact. These businesses contribute to the state's economy while also playing a critical role in community development through various corporate social responsibility (CSR) initiatives. These initiatives often focus on healthcare, education, and environmental sustainability, reflecting the businesses' deep-rooted commitment to the welfare of their communities.

Innovation in Gujarat does not stop at community and family-oriented business practices. The state is also a leader in adopting new technologies and sustainable practices across various sectors. In agriculture, for instance, Gujarat is pioneering sustainable and ethical practices that significantly increase efficiency and productivity while ensuring environmental conservation. Techniques like drip irrigation and organic farming are prominent, showcasing the state's commitment to sustainable agricultural development.

The diamond industry in Gujarat, renowned globally, serves as a prime example of how traditional businesses are evolving to meet modern ethical standards. The adoption of technologies such as blockchain for enhancing transparency and trust in the diamond trade underscores a broader trend across Gujarat's industries where ethical practices are increasingly becoming embedded in the business operations.

Furthermore, the role of women in business in Gujarat is evolving. Women are increasingly taking on leadership roles and driving the state's economic growth. This shift is not only transforming the business landscape but also challenging the traditional norms and providing a model for gender equality in business.

Gujarat's commitment to sustainability is also evident in its approach to tourism. Responsible tourism practices in Gujarat aim to minimize the environmental impact while maximizing social and economic benefits for local communities. These practices are not only enhancing the visitor experience but also preserving the state's rich cultural and natural heritage for future generations.

As businesses in Gujarat navigate the complexities of the global market, they remain deeply rooted in local values. This balance of local and global is a defining characteristic of Gujarat's business culture, providing a competitive edge in the international arena. The state's businesses demonstrate that it is possible to remain committed to local values while embracing global business practices, a balance that is crucial in today's interconnected world.

Looking ahead, Gujarat is poised to continue its journey towards global leadership in ethical business practices. The state's model of integrating ethics with business is a blueprint that can inspire businesses worldwide. The ongoing commitment to innovation, sustainability, and community-oriented practices is likely to keep Gujarat at the forefront of economic development, setting a benchmark for others to follow.

In summary, Gujarat's path in the business world is marked by a blend of rich traditions and modern innovations. This unique combination is what makes the state not just a leader in India but an exemplary figure on the global stage. As the world moves towards more ethical and sustainable business practices, Gujarat's journey offers valuable insights and a hopeful vision of the future, where integrity and prosperity go hand in hand.

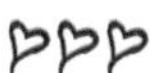

Citation And References

This book represents the culmination of extensive research and meticulous analysis, incorporating a diverse range of sources, including numerous books, scholarly studies, and personal experiences. Additionally, I have scoured various websites to gather relevant information and data essential for the compilation of this work. I have taken every precaution to ensure the accuracy of the information presented and have diligently cited all sources to acknowledge their contributions.

Despite these efforts, the possibility of inadvertent errors remains. I deeply value the insights of my readers and appreciate any feedback that can help identify and rectify such inaccuracies. I encourage you to bring any discrepancies to my attention.

Your feedback is not only welcome but crucial, as it will aid in correcting current editions and enhancing the content of future ones. I am committed to maintaining the highest standards of accuracy and reliability in my work and thank you for your support and understanding.

Additionally, I firmly uphold the principle of freedom of speech and expression as guaranteed under Article 19(1)(a) of the Constitution of India, and I respect the diverse viewpoints and expressions of all readers.

ϷϷϷ

Other Books Of The Author

1. Empowering Minds: A Journey into Women's Self-Discovery and Power
2. The Dynamics of Motivation: Catalyzing Thought into Action
3. Meditation and Mental Well Being: The Path to Inner Peace and Clarity
4. The Psychology of Child Education: Nurturing Future Generations
5. Ethical Enlightenment: A Modern Guide to Living with Integrity
6. Voices of Empowerment: Stories of Women Rising Against Odds
7. Social Psychology in Everyday Life: Understanding Human Connections
8. The Essence of Motivational Speaking: Inspiring Change in Others
9. Balancing Acts: Women, Work, and the Will to Lead
10. Guiding with Grace: Raising Children with Compassion and Awareness
11. The Power of Positive Aging: Embracing Life After Fifty
12. Building Resilient Communities: Social Work in Action
13. The Ethical Educator: Principles for Teaching and Learning
14. From Insight to Impact: Social Psychology for a Better World
15. The Ethics of Empathy: A Guide to Ethical Living
16. The Science of Empowering the Self: Navigating Life's Challenges with Psychological Wisdom
17. The Mindful Conscious Leader: Meditation Techniques for Modern Management
18. Pioneering Spirit: Women's Pathways to Leadership and Empowerment
19. Feeling to Healing: The Role of Emotional Intelligence in Child Development
20. Transformative Talks and Words of Inspiration: Insights into Motivational Oratory

ঌঌঌ

Contact

Dr. Minakshi Bansal
Social Activist
Ahmedabad, Gujarat, Bharat
minakshiindiag20@yahoo.com

❥❥❥

|| LOKAHA SAMASTHAHA SUKHINO BHAVANTU ||

• 131 •